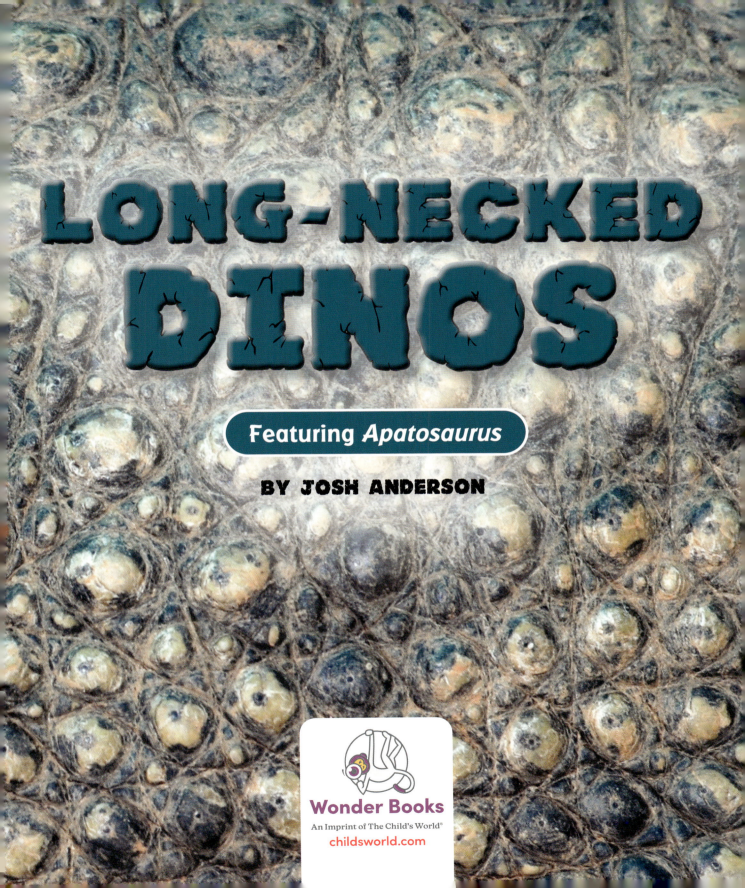

LONG-NECKED DINOS

Featuring *Apatosaurus*

BY JOSH ANDERSON

Wonder Books
An Imprint of The Child's World®
childsworld.com

Published by The Child's World®
800-599-READ • www.childsworld.com

Copyright © 2023 by The Child's World®
All rights reserved. No part of this book may be reproduced or utilized in any form or by any means without written permission from the publisher.

Photography Credits
Cover: ©Warpaint / Shutterstock; page 1: ©Pan Xunbin/Shutterstock; page 5: ©Warpaintcobra/Getty Images; page 6: ©Hulton Archive/Stringer/Getty Images; page 9: ©Stan Godlewski/ZUMA Press/Newscom; page 10: ©Elenarts108/Getty Images; page 12: ©Daniel Eskridge/Shutterstock; page 13: ©Daniel Eskridge/Shutterstock; page 14: ©Matt Cardy/Stringer/Getty Images; page 15: ©Bettmann/Contributor/Getty Images; page 16: ©Tuul & Bruno Morandi/Getty Images; page 16: ©Julio Francisco; page 17: ©Julio Francisco; page 19: ©Ryan Sutherland/Bureau of Land Management–Utah; page 21: ©James St. John/Flickr

ISBN Information
9781503865280 (Reinforced Library Binding)
9781503865907 (Portable Document Format)
9781503866744 (Online Multi-user eBook)
9781503867581 (Electronic Publication)

LCCN 2022940986

Printed in the United States of America

About the Author

Josh Anderson has published more than 50 books for children and young adults. His two sons, Leo and Dane, are the greatest joys in his life. Josh's hobbies include coaching youth basketball, no-holds-barred games of Exploding Kittens, reading, and family movie nights. His favorite dinosaur is a secret he'll never share!

CONTENTS

Digging for Bones...4

What We Know...11

Keep Searching...18

Glossary...22
Wonder More...23
Learn More...24
Index...24

CHAPTER 1

Digging for Bones

Pretend you can time travel to a prehistoric age.... You've gone back about 155 million years to the Rocky Mountains. Nearby, you spot a long tail on the ground. You follow it with your eyes . . . and follow it . . . and follow it. It belongs to a dinosaur called *Apatosaurus* (uh-pat-uh-SAWR-uss). It is the longest creature you've ever seen. Its neck alone is close to 20 feet (6 meters) long! It is eating the leaves of a nearby bush. The dinosaur sees you. It thinks you are a predator and starts to swing its huge tail in your direction. Thankfully, you're able to get away in time!

How do we know so much about a creature that lived many millions of years before the first humans? The simple answer: SCIENCE! Let's learn more!

Many people call *Apatosaurus* by another name—*Brontosaurus*—but the two dinosaurs have slight differences.

Othniel Marsh identified dozens of new types of animals throughout his career, many of them dinosaurs.

Humans have been studying *Apatosaurus* for more than 140 years. *Apatosaurus* bones were first discovered in 1877 in Morrison, Colorado. Famous **paleontologist** Othniel Charles Marsh was the first to study them. Marsh named the dinosaur *Apatosaurus*. The name means "**deceptive** lizard." Marsh thought *Apatosaurus* was deceptive because its bones looked like those of a reptile called a mosasaur.

The first *Apatosaurus* skeleton put on display was at the American Museum of Natural History in New York. Scientists discovered the bones in the 1890s. But it took until 1905 to get the dinosaur ready for viewing. You can still see it there today!

Scientists disagreed for years about what an *Apatosaurus* head looked like. That's because a skull was not found until long after the dinosaur's first bones were. Original models of *Apatosaurus* may have had the heads of other dinosaurs by mistake.

In 1978, an *Apatosaurus* skull was found in a museum basement. Scientists examined the **fossil**. They learned that *Apatosaurus* had long, thin, peg-like teeth. Museums around the world changed their models of Apatosaurus after this.

Scientists learn about dinosaurs both by what they find and by what they don't find. For example, *Apatosaurus* fossils usually aren't discovered in bone beds. Bone beds are groups of bones containing several skeletons of the same dinosaur. When scientists find bone beds, they can make the guess that an animal lived in a group. Since *Apatosaurus* is usually found alone, it probably lived a **solitary** life.

Apatosaurus had around 56 teeth. It used them like a rake to gather leaves and grass into its mouth.

CHAPTER 2

What We Know

Apatosaurus was a kind of dinosaur called a sauropod. Like other sauropods, *Apatosaurus* was large with a very long neck and tail. All sauropods stood on four legs. They were plant-eaters. *Apatosaurus* was heavier than many sauropods. Some scientists believe it could have weighed more than 90,000 pounds (40,823 kilograms).

When It Lived: 155 million years ago – The Late Jurassic Period

Where It Lived: North America; low hills

First Discovered: 1877, Colorado

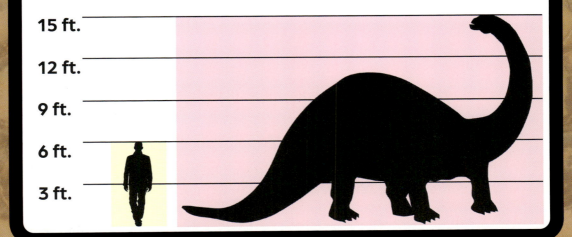

Even though it had a long neck, *Apatosaurus* likely didn't eat from the treetops. It probably grazed on plants and bushes near the ground. It probably swallowed stones too. The stones would have helped move the leafy food through its long body. *Apatosaurus* probably ate more than 800 pounds (363 kg) of food per day in order to have enough energy.

FUN FACTS

- An *Apatosaurus* brain was about the size of a computer mouse.
- Some scientists think *Apatosaurus* lived up to 100 years.
- The sound of an *Apatosaurus* whipping its tail might've been louder than a cannon!
- *Apatosaurus* may have reached its full-grown, adult size by around 20 years old.
- *Apatosaurus* hatched from eggs that were likely a foot (30 centimeters) wide or more!

THEN AND NOW

It was once thought that *Apatosaurus* spent a lot of time in the water. The water would've helped the creature's joints handle the weight of its body. But now scientists believe the dinosaur's large head and neck balanced its huge tail. The balance provided enough support for the dinosaur to live mostly on land.

Apatosaurus had thick, pillar-like legs, similar to an elephant's legs.

Dippy is a full-size model of a *Diplodocus*. It is displayed at the Natural History Museum in London, England.

Apatosaurus wasn't the only long-necked dinosaur. Here are a couple of others from the ancient world:

Amargasaurus (uh-marg-uh-SAWR-uss) was much smaller than *Apatosaurus*. It roamed Earth millions of years later too. It had very long spines along its back. These may have supported two webs of skin that looked like a ship's sails.

Diplodocus (dih-PLAHD-uh-kuss) was even longer than *Apatosaurus*. It is the longest dinosaur ever pieced together as a full skeleton. *Diplodocus* and *Apatosaurus* lived at the same time. Their bones have even been found in the same locations.

UP FOR DEBATE

In the late 1800s, bone collectors often sent fossils to Othniel Charles Marsh for examination. Marsh named many of the dinosaurs we know today. He first identified *Apatosaurus* and *Brontosaurus* (brahn-tuh-SAWR-uss) as two different **species**. Scientists later discovered they were the same dinosaur. The name *Apatosaurus* stuck. But recent discoveries have convinced some scientists that they actually are different species. Some scientists now consider *Brontosaurus* a separate dinosaur.

APATOSAURUS
(uh-pat-uh-SAWR-uss)

Length: 75 feet (23 m)

Height: 15 feet (4.6 m)

Weight: 40,000 pounds (18,144 kg)

Weakness: Slow-moving, 7–9 miles (11–14 kilometers) per hour

Best Weapon or Defense: Long tail that might've been used as a whip

BRACHIOSAURUS
(bray-kee-oh-SAWR-uss)

Length: 75 feet (23 m)

Height: 40 feet (12 m)

Weight: 120,000 pounds (54,431 kg)

Weakness: Slow-moving, 10 miles (16 km) per hour

Best Weapon or Defense: Massive size made it an unlikely target for predators

CHAPTER 3

Keep Searching

Scientists are learning new things about dinosaurs every day. A lot of what we know about *Apatosaurus* has been discovered in recent years.

A 2011 discovery of an *Apatosaurus* skull was very important. The skull had some of its neck bones attached. Scientists compared these bones with another set. This comparison allowed scientists to determine that *Brontosaurus* was likely a separate dinosaur from *Apatosaurus* (see page 15).

New inventions help scientists learn more about fossils that are millions of years old.

In 2014, a group from the Museum of Western Colorado saw part of a bone sticking up through some rock. They didn't think there was anything special about the bone at first. But as the team **excavated** it, they realized it was huge—and in one piece. The bone measured 6 feet, 7 inches (2 m) long. It is the longest *Apatosaurus* leg bone ever discovered.

Where will the next major discovery about *Apatosaurus* come from? Perhaps someone reading this book will one day teach us something new about these giants of the past.

The average *Apatosaurus* leg bone was around six feet (1.8 m) tall.

GLOSSARY

deceptive (dih-SEP-tihv): misleading; not what it seems

excavate (EK-skeh-vayt): to make a hole by digging

fossil (FAH-sul): the remains or traces of plants and animals that lived long ago

paleontologist (pay-lee-on-TOL-uh-jist): a scientist who studies plants and animals that lived millions of years ago

predator (PREH-duh-tur): an animal that hunts or kills another animal for food

prehistoric (pree-hiss-TORE-ick): belonging to a period in a time before written history

solitary (SAHL-uh-tayr-ee): being or living alone

species (SPEE-sheez): a group of living things that are able to reproduce

WONDER MORE

Think About It: *Apatosaurus* could stretch 75 feet (23 m) from its head to the tip of its tail. That's longer than two full-sized school buses! How might it have felt for one end of its body to be so far from the other?

Talk About It: Imagine being a *Brachiosaurus*, looking out over the world from 40 feet (12 m) in the air. Ask your family or friends how the world might look different from up there.

Write About It: Take another look at pages 16 and 17. It's unlikely that plant-eaters *Apatosaurus* and *Brachiosaurus* would've fought. But both were sometimes attacked by *Allosaurus* (al-oh-SAWR-uss), a meat-eater that lived at the same time. Write about how the two long-necks might've teamed up to defend themselves from *Allosaurus*.

MESOZOIC ERA

Triassic Period	Jurassic Period	Cretaceous Period
201–252 Million Years Ago	145–201 Million Years Ago	66–145 Million Years Ago

LEARN MORE

BOOKS

Carr, Aaron. *Apatosaurus*. New York: AV2, 2021.

Kelly, Erin Suzanne. *Dinosaurs*. New York: Children's Press, 2021.

Sabelko, Rebecca. *Apatosaurus*. Minneapolis: Bellwether Media, 2021.

WEBSITES

Visit our website for links about *Apatosaurus*: **childsworld.com/links**

Note to Parents, Caregivers, Teachers, and Librarians: We routinely verify our web links to make sure they are safe and active sites. So encourage your readers to check them out!

INDEX

Amargasaurus, 15
American Museum of Natural History, 7

bone beds, 8
bones, 7–8, 15, 18
Brachiosaurus, 17
Brontosaurus, 5, 15, 18

Diplodocus, 14–15

Jurassic Period, 11

Marsh, Othniel Charles, 6–7, 15
Morrison, Colorado, 7
Museum of Western Colorado, 20

North America, 11

Rocky Mountains, 4

sauropods, 11

teeth, 8–9

water, 13